The Rivered Earth

The Rivered Earth

VIKRAM SETH

HAMISH HAMILTON
CANADA

HAMISH HAMILTON CANADA

Published by the Penguin Group

Penguin Group (Canada), 90 Eglinton Avenue East, Suite 700, Toronto, Ontario, Canada M4P 2Y3
    (a division of Pearson Canada Inc.)

Penguin Group (USA) Inc., 375 Hudson Street, New York, New York 10014, U.S.A.
Penguin Books Ltd, 80 Strand, London WC2R 0RL, England
Penguin Ireland, 25 St Stephen's Green, Dublin 2, Ireland (a division of Penguin Books Ltd)
Penguin Group (Australia), 250 Camberwell Road, Camberwell, Victoria 3124, Australia
    (a division of Pearson Australia Group Pty Ltd)
Penguin Books India Pvt Ltd, 11 Community Centre, Panchsheel Park, New Delhi – 110 017, India
Penguin Group (NZ), 67 Apollo Drive, Rosedale, Auckland 0632, New Zealand
    (a division of Pearson New Zealand Ltd)
Penguin Books (South Africa) (Pty) Ltd, 24 Sturdee Avenue, Rosebank, Johannesburg 2196, South Africa

Penguin Books Ltd, Registered Offices: 80 Strand, London WC2R 0RL, England

Published in Hamish Hamilton Canada hardcover by Penguin Group (Canada), a division of Pearson Canada
Inc., 2011. Simultaneously published in the U.K. by Hamish Hamilton, an imprint of Penguin Books.

1 2 3 4 5 6 7 8 9 10   (RRD)

LIBRARY AND ARCHIVES CANADA CATALOGUING IN PUBLICATION

Seth, Vikram, 1952–
    The rivered earth / Vikram Seth.

Poems.

ISBN 978-0-670-06458-8

    I. Title.

PR9499.3.S39R59 2011   821'.914   C2011-905330-6

British Library Cataloguing in Publication data available

Visit the Penguin Group (Canada) website at www.penguin.ca

Special and corporate bulk purchase rates available; please see
www.penguin.ca/corporatesales or call 1-800-810-3104, ext. 2477 or 2474

To Alec Roth and Philippe Honoré

Contents

General Introduction

Some time ago, when I was 'between books', I took part in a project that resulted in several remarkable works of music – involving, from my pen, four very different libretti. Apart from the texts themselves, published here, each with its own brief introduction, I thought it might be of interest to write a more general account of this project, which was unusual in several senses: it was a collaboration between a writer, a composer and a violinist; it developed over four years, with a work produced each year; it took place with the encouragement and within the constraints of three festivals and, indeed, communities; the libretti touched upon three civilizations, Chinese, European and Indian; and much of the work – both literary and musical – was created in a house with rich literary and musical associations, a house on the River Nadder in Wiltshire.

The project was called 'Confluences', but because that name sounds a bit technical, I sought a more vivid title for this book and for the four libretti as a whole. The composer suggested 'the rivered earth', a phrase from the last of the libretti, suggestive perhaps of the beauty of our common planet. In fact, the two halves of the phrase encompass the four texts, since the first begins with the image of the moon reflected in a great river, and the last ends with the image of the blue earth spinning through time and space.

The composer Alec Roth, the violinist Philippe Honoré and I were standing in a red room with a large black piano, anticipating the arrival of the directors of the Salisbury and Chelsea festivals.

What we needed was a project for the coming year that would enthuse all three of us and would kindle the interest of the directors. But our various suggestions were all over the place – from unaccompanied choirs to the solo violin, from community choruses to chamber orchestras, from violin and piano sonatas to song-cycles, from pieces for instrumental ensembles to grand oratorios. What we were agreed upon was that crucial to the works would be Philippe's violin and Alec's composition and my words – and therefore the human voice, which has always been at the heart of Alec's music, even his instrumental music. But we could settle on none of the various alternatives.

About five minutes before our guests were due to arrive, I said, 'Let's ask for it all.'

'What do you mean?' said Philippe.

'I mean, let's suggest some sort of grand plan where each year we would undertake to create a new work and they would undertake to support its creation and performance. It's now summer 2005. So what about something for each of the four years from 2006 to 2009?'

'Four years?' said Alec. 'It's hard enough getting funding for one. Festival finances have always been in a precarious state. They stagger along from one year to the next: almost all their funding and fund-raising is on an annual basis.'

'Well, don't festivals ever commission composers or projects for more than a single year?'

'It's very rare. I can't think of an example of it, offhand.'

'So how come there's any continuity in what a festival offers from one year to another?'

'There isn't much. It's all a bit ad hoc. The moment the actual festival is over, they start thinking of what to do for the next. I suppose the overall vision of the director gives it some sort of continuity.'

'Haven't you ever had a commission for more than a single year?'

'No.'

'Well, let's ask for it. In fact, let's insist on it. And let's try to get a guarantee right from the beginning that they'll follow it through. I can't imagine anything more killing to any kind of long-term vision than the business of applying for a commission a year at a time and the uncertainty of whether it'll come through.'

'That's how it is in the real world.'

'I didn't know that. And some good ideas come out of ignorance. So let's give it a try.'

'There's nothing to be lost,' said Philippe. 'It would be fantastic to have a new piece to work on each year for the next four years.'

'They'll never agree,' said Alec.

An hour or so later we were looking at each other in amazement. Not only had Jo Metcalf Shore and Stewart Collins not blanched at the idea, they'd been intrigued. They had asked us to write up a proposal: ideas, forms, forces, venues, costs. But it was clear to them from the start that they'd have to get a third festival to join them to make it possible. Some time later they met Richard Hawley, who had recently been appointed director of the Lichfield Festival. Now that they had a troika, they set about trying to get funding. Eventually both the Arts Council and the PRS Foundation expressed their enthusiasm and guaranteed funding for three years, and the various festival boards signalled their approval – presumably assuming that funding for the fourth year would somehow work out.

But all this took quite some time – many months, in fact. By now Alec, Philippe and I were champing at the bit and had half given up hope. Indeed, by the time the confirmation of the project did come through, it was so late that I couldn't create a new work for the first year. I was in Delhi, Alec was in Durham – and there was hardly any time to consult, let alone write. In the event, we had to think of a different solution.

Yet we were all conscious of how unusual it was that our project existed at all. We dubbed it 'Confluences' to indicate the variety of ideas and geographies and forces that merged within it. The other reason for the name was that it implied a voyage downstream, with other tributaries (performers, influences, ideas, and so on) joining en route.

Our brief each year was to create a work of about twenty minutes for voice, violin and other forces. It would be given three performances over the course of a few weeks in summer – one at each of the three festivals: Salisbury, Chelsea and Lichfield, in that order. The first three years would touch upon China, Europe and India respectively; the theme for the fourth year was to be left open – to the suggestions of (among others) our audiences, to natural development from within the works themselves, and to any extraneous inspiration that might strike. The venues would be large local churches with good acoustics and lines of sight, as well as Lichfield and Salisbury cathedrals. The forces would range, depending on the year, from small ensembles to an orchestra to professional choirs to massed amateur choruses of men, women and children.

In fact, the works turned out to be between forty minutes and an hour long, and far richer and more complex than we had imagined. The first year produced a song-cycle for tenor, violin, harp and guitar, *Songs in Time of War*. The second year saw six pieces for unaccompanied professional chorus – *Shared*

Ground – interleaved with five pieces for unaccompanied violin – *Ponticelli* – something like a suite dovetailed into a motet, but composed so that they could also be performed separately. The third year produced an oratorio, *The Traveller*, for violin and tenor soloists, large amateur chorus (including children's choir) and string orchestra plus harp and percussion. For the final year, Alec created three separate but related works: a cycle of seven songs for tenor and piano called *Seven Elements*, a seven-movement sonata-like suite for violin and piano called the *Seven Elements Suite*, plus a short coda, *The Hermit on the Ice*, for all three performers.

Being indolent by nature, if there is one thing I hate, it is making an effort for nothing. It would be more than frustrating to write a halfway decent libretto only to find that the composer had made a botch of the music. Alec had set my poems in the past, as well as written an opera, *Arion and the Dolphin*, to a libretto of mine, so I was confident he would produce something good. But I could not have expected anything as magical as what emerged. The works he produced over these four years are profound, various, moving, imperishable. I am more privileged than I can say that my words provided him with some of the inspiration to create them. Let me leave a hostage to fortune and state that Alec Roth's works – and not just these but others – are among the finest ever created by an English composer. And part of the reason that they are not better known and more widely enjoyed is because Alec is so hopeless at self-promotion.

It was others who got hold of the BBC and told them of the reception and reviews the first year's première had received. Roger Wright of Radio 3 arranged for the final performance (in Lichfield Cathedral) to be recorded and broadcast, and this continued for the remaining three years. Thanks to sponsorship from an anonymous donor, the first of the works, *Songs in Time of War*, was recorded in 2008; the second, *Shared Ground*, is due for release in 2011.* (The performers are the same as at the festivals.) One hopes that CDs of the other works will follow. Indeed, because of the way the themes of the works, verbal and (in particular) musical, develop from year to year, echoing and reflecting what has gone before, it would be an enriching experience to hear the works performed one after another over the course of a day, or perhaps two evenings. The works form a family and, for all their differences, a close one.

The experience for me of creating these four texts, entirely in verse, was full of variety: a mixture of translation and original creation, drawing from a range of personal experience as well as the influence of others – and the consciousness that what I was writing had to be sung. One text was written many years ago – translations from Classical Chinese, a language monosyllabic in nature. One consisted of translations from Indian languages, which are far from monosyllabic, together with six original poems, three iambic, three trochaic, in a variety of line-lengths. For one I used another poet's forms as a template for my own inspiration. And for one I wrote eight poems in a variety of rhymed and unrhymed forms of my choosing. I talk about these in my brief introductions to the individual libretti.

Alec and I usually consulted closely at the beginning of this process before I went off to do my thing. But this was some-times quite frustrating for him. Once he sat in my house in Salisbury, cooling his heels for a week because I couldn't put myself in the right frame of mind to think about the project. We sat down and talked about it but didn't get anywhere. We

---

* SIGCD124 (*Songs in Time of War*); SIGCD270 (*Shared Ground*); signumrecords.com

then poured ourselves a glass of wine and went for a walk in the water-meadow past a bare oak tree, which was surrounded, owing to heavy rains, by a pool; we stood there, staring at what looked like the tree's roots but were actually its leafless branches reflected in the water. Some months later this image would lead to the poems of *Shared Ground*. The next year he wrote me a series of elaborate memoranda that helped me feel my way to my theme; and it was his strength of feeling for some verses of the Dhammapada that gave them such a prominent role in *The Traveller*. Even after I handed him the draft of a particular libretto, there were discussions, cullings, rearrangements, suggestions for amendment – and in one case even the request that I go back and produce something entirely different.

Words are all very well, but the success of a musical work lies in its music – and, on the whole, Alec's main task began after mine had ended – and Philippe's main task after Alec's. Before writing this introduction I talked to both of them in order to be able to cast some light on these later stages, and even occasionally on the actual process of composition, which strikes me as being as mysterious as that of writing. The consultation between them, the choice of the other performers, the involvement of the festivals and the local community, the programming for the first half of the concerts, the changes to the music made in the aftermath of actual performances: all these were essential aspects of the project, and because Philippe and Alec talk with great insight about them, I have set their thoughts down largely in their own words.

As a composer, Alec writes with particular venues in mind – their acoustic and visual and even dramatic possibilities. In the third year, our piece (based on India) was to be performed in Salisbury Cathedral. While we were still discussing possible themes for the libretto and before I had written a single word of it, Alec wrote me a note which he headed 'Memorandum 1 from AR to VS':

> I woke up this morning with an interesting sound in my head. Remember how the Advent Procession begins? Everyone stands up and faces West. All the lights are extinguished; it's pitch dark. Suddenly, quite high up a single candle flame appears. One by one other candles are lit from the first one and move out. In each aisle, North and South, a procession begins and the light spreads down the nave. Imagine this in sonic terms: darkness/silence; the sound of the solo violin; gradually its notes spread to other violins (or voices?); the sound, now a texture of overlapping harmonies, spreads out to envelop the whole building. This would be a powerfully dramatic beginning. Isn't there a verse in the Bhagavad Gita where Krishna says something like, 'I am the spark that brings life to all living things'? . . .

Similarly – and again this gives his music something almost indefinably personal – Alec writes with particular musicians in mind, not for, say, a general tenor or general violinist. He enjoyed this greatly over the course of the four years, because we were lucky to get wonderful performers. *Songs in Time of War* was sung by the tenor Mark Padmore with Philippe Honoré on the violin, Alison Nicholls on the harp and Morgan Szymanski on the guitar. *Shared Ground* was sung by the choir Ex Cathedra conducted by Jeffrey Skidmore, while *Ponticelli*, which interleaved its movements, was played by Philippe. In the third year, *The Traveller* was sung by Mark Padmore, together with large local choruses, including children's chorus. The solo violinist was Philippe and the orchestra was the Britten Sinfonia. In the final year, *Seven Elements* was sung by the tenor James Gilchrist with Rustem Hayroudinoff on the piano, the *Seven Elements Suite* was performed by Philippe and Rustem, and *The Hermit on the Ice* by all three.

Because Philippe was one of the three equal initiating partners in the project, and it was understood from the start that he would play a crucial role in the music, Alec wrote more for the violin over these four years than he could ever have imagined he would. I talked to Philippe about this.

VS: What was it like to have four years of Alec's music to play?

PH: I feel I was really lucky. You know what I think of Alec as a composer. Sometimes, as a musician, one works so hard in an orchestra or at sessions work, where you have no choice in what is being played, that there's a danger of getting a bit stale, even treating music as a humdrum profession. What can keep one's pleasure in music fresh is if one is able to play in smaller ensembles or to do solo work. And best of all, of course, is to work on something written specially for you, with your style and tastes and abilities in mind. So it was great to work with Alec's music – with a new piece every year. And of course frustrating sometimes.

VS: Frustrating?

PH: Well, I sometimes thought I didn't get enough of it! I was particularly frustrated in the first year, when we did *Songs in Time of War* sung by tenor, with a slightly unusual setting: violin as well as both harp and guitar – two plucked instruments similar in many ways – and no real bass instrument. The texture was very similar – though it actually worked really well. Talking of similar textures: there was pizzicato for the violin as well; in fact there's one number where I play pizzicato but the harp and guitar don't come in. Alec had also worked with me on various effects, and he used some of them. I especially remember what I call the pigeon noise – a sort of fluttering of feathers – it's a particular bowing effect. But anyway, it was an ensemble piece that year and the violin was not used as a main voice or a particularly important voice. It was merely another one.

VS: You did get that solo in 'The Old Cypress Tree' – that dance which Alec says is at the heart of things – a sort of reminder of when life was good and full of ordinary pleasures, before war destroyed it all. Though I admit you received it pretty late and it was sort of iffy whether it would be ready for the première. You got it one day before the performance, if I recall.

PH: That's right. So I don't know how well I played it in Salisbury. Chelsea was better, though, and Lichfield OK. Of course, Alec always made changes between performances; they were never exactly the same. He might change the voicing here or the pitch there – or tweak something else. Which was good in a way: it kept us on our toes.

VS: In the second year you got *Ponticelli* – the suite for solo violin whose movements were interleaved with those of *Shared Ground*. Alec dedicated it to you and – not to embarrass you – the reviewer in *The Times* said you played it magically.

PH: Well, the work itself was amazing. Of course when I practised it, I played it as a suite or partita, and it hangs together really well. In fact, it has the same number of movements –

five – as Bach's D Minor Partita, which ends with the Chaconne. Alec's piece too ends with a very rich and complex movement. There are common features with the Chaconne: not only melody but also chords, two voices, double-stops, etc. And unique features too, of course: that plucking while I'm playing arco, for example; very challenging. It's a tremendous addition to the solo violin repertoire.

Alec said he didn't want to echo the Chaconne too much, and I can't think of any direct references. But the way the variations in the last movement develop is similar to how the Chaconne develops – for example, with all that bariolage (is that a word in English? – we use it in French) across the strings.

You delivered your words very late that year, so Alec began composing the solo violin stuff quite early. I remember him coming to the Queen Elizabeth Hall, as the Royal Festival Hall was being refurbished, and our finding a dressing room at the back to talk things through between one of my rehearsals and a concert. We spent more than an hour discussing the music and I made various suggestions; but by then, of course, the piece was already quite advanced.

VS: Is there anything you're not quite happy with?

PH: I'm not too sure about the use of the mute in the first movement, now that I've listened to it on the recording for radio. In the crescendo, the mute prevents it from going beyond a certain volume of sound. But that's just an opinion.*

---

* Alec has subsequently made his instruction for this movement ('Flat Bridge') more flexible; it is now up to the violinist whether to use the wooden mute or not.

VS: Coming to the third year and *The Traveller* . . .

PH: Well, in the third year, Alec took a huge amount on and I felt he short-changed the violin. You gave him too many words, Vikram – and of course the words had to be sung and there was only so much space for the violin.

VS: Yes, I'm sorry. I didn't actually give him the words: I selected some texts and told him to cull them. But he greedily grabbed them all.

PH: Do you know, if there's one tune that I remember straight-away when I think of the project, it would be that theme in the solo violin meditation in year three, which appeared again in the violin suite in year four. Strange to think that it almost didn't exist. In fact, in Salisbury it didn't – when the work was premièred and reviewed.

VS: If it hadn't existed it would have been a tragedy. The reviewer in *The Times*, who came to the Salisbury performance, and who praised your playing of the Ysaÿe solo violin sonata – 'dispatched with fire and pluck' (nice pun there) – mentioned that he was disappointed that in the new work, you, as the supposed 'travel-ler', didn't have much to do on your own.

PH: I actually think that review made Alec decide to write something specifically for the violin – and, though he was very busy, compose it in time for Chelsea. I think he felt bad – but then went on to create something wonderful. [*Philippe pauses, then goes on:*] You know, I think, with Alec – though he has written a string quartet now, and instrumental works, and that nocturne for harp and violin that Alison and I played –

writing for the violin doesn't come naturally to him, and I don't think that that's what he wants to do first. He's very much in the voice and choral tradition. That's where he's at his most comfortable and of course singers love what he writes for them. And librettists too, I suppose, because the words are set so clearly. But it's a shame that he doesn't write more for strings because I think it would be fantastic. When he puts his mind to it, it really works. That Meditation was perfect. For me, of course, it was a great relief that I could say something individually for once instead of just being part of a big noise. And maybe the adrenalin brought about by the stress of its newness helped my playing! But it was also very good for the balance of the piece itself to have that reflection without words.

When he got around to writing it and sent me the score, I read it on my own at first. I then went to rehearse it with him; this was just two days before the Chelsea Festival. 'Oh God, why did you put me so high up there on the E string?' I asked him. He said – and this is typical of Alec, who composes for the sound of particular performers – 'Because when you play up there I find it beautiful and I wanted to use it.' Unfortunately I had – and still have – a wolf note on my violin that affects all the Cs and particularly the high ones. It was fine that year, but sometimes when I play that piece it drives me crazy. I know they say that only good violins have wolf notes, but . . .

VS: I can't understand how wolf notes can drive you crazy, Philippe, when you didn't seem to be distracted by the G-sharp hum from the fused fluorescent lighting in Salisbury Cathedral when you played the solo Ysaÿe.

PH: Hmm. Actually, it was very distracting before I began playing; but you just get on with it. Between movements it was a bit disturbing. But I love the Ysaÿe, and it was great to play it in that space, with some distance and resonance.

VS: In the fourth year you got plenty to do – with that violin and piano suite.

PH: Yes! But we had to fight for it. Alec wanted to write it for violin and guitar.

VS: I don't think Alec is in love with the piano. He thinks it a bit of a bully.

PH: Well, he writes well for it – in his own idiom – with an open texture. You know, it may be great to write for unusual combinations of instruments, but if you write for normal forces, like violin and piano, your pieces are much more likely to be repeated and heard. I really longed for something that I would be able to continue to play after the whole project was over.

VS: So we bullied poor Alec when he brought up the question of the guitar. I remember making it clear on the patio that day that I wasn't having it. My muse would go on strike.

PH: Perhaps there was a bit less novelty in the violin and piano piece of the fourth year than in the solo violin suite of the second year. But that was right in a way: themes from earlier years were brought in to weave things together, to give a sense of closure. The Meditation theme came in. So did the *Dies Irae* semiquavers and double-stops from the Ysaÿe. It gave me a lot of pleasure when I came to play it. In general, in an instrumental work by Alec, things always look a bit bare and almost unfinished on paper. There's no articulation, hardly any dynamic instructions – even less than in Bach! – not too many tempi indications either, and he writes in normal notation without the usual twenty-first-century markings. It looks easy but it's very deceptive. You have to explore it and understand it yourself. The moment I start to work on it, I begin to find things. The piece starts taking shape and grows richer and richer musically and emotionally, and this process never really stops.

A few weeks after I talked to Philippe, in the course of a conversation with Alec, I brought up the question of the violin. Had he ever played it?

AR: Not since I was at school and people begged me to stop. I tried the cello too, but not for long.

VS: So how do you write for strings? Especially something like the suite for unaccompanied violin that you produced in the second year?

AR: It's the same as when I compose for guitar – or any other instrument I don't play. The process goes something like this: I write a few sketches; then I take them to the performer, and we start playing around with them – and that's how I start learning about the instrument and what works well with it and what doesn't. The advantage of this initial ignorance is that you sometimes come across something that is quite original in conception, but which doesn't fall under the well-worn path of the fingers – doesn't sit, so to speak, and in some cases is physically impossible to play. When something like this happened, Philippe would say, 'I can't do it exactly like that but I could do it like this or like this,' and we found a way of adapting it to make it work. That was really satisfying for both of us because his ideas got into it. And over the four years, I've got better at writing for the violin and for strings in general.

Or else the inspiration might come more directly from hearing something he did. I remember asking him in a sort of workshop session to play the open strings bowed. The sonority he produced made a huge impression on me, and I began looking at the effect of an open string being played as a pulsed drone while the string below it or above it was being played melodically; and then moving up from one string to another in the same manner. I use that idea for the first movement of *Ponticelli*, the suite for solo violin. It's not like anything I've ever written before and I still think it's the best of the movements.

VS: I like the last movement best myself – it's got tremendous energy and compulsiveness.

AR [*laughing*]: Philippe was always looking for a challenge. So that's where I thought I'd keep him quiet with technical matters – but I was astonished by what he did. That last movement was full of all sorts of shenanigans: left-hand pizzicato as well as lots of right-hand pizz, multinote chords, harmonics, the lot. And he played it as if all that was no problem at all – and got to the heart of the music, to the dance of it.

VS: For me – and for Philippe too – one of the most beautiful moments of all was the Meditation by the violin towards the end of *The Traveller*. Which, of course, almost didn't get written.

AR [*looking slightly guilty*]: Er, yes, it wasn't there in the first performance, in Salisbury. Let me explain. I was writing the music in a very artificial order that year, not at all in the sequence of the libretto itself. I had to do all the children's choruses first – they needed a very long rehearsal time since they sang from memory. I gave them their parts just after Christmas, I think. Second, all the chorus work: the amateurs had to start learning it in the spring. Then, the solo voice for Mark Padmore. The orchestra next: a month before the première. Apart from this, there was the physical effort of producing all those parts. So with regard to the violin I rather lost my way. I saw the violin as 'the traveller', but the voices tended to dominate it whenever they appeared together because, well, they had the words. It was only after hearing the first performance that I realized that something was missing: a passage without words, an extended instrumental meditation, a fantasia for solo violin at the end of the last section. I thought, 'How on earth will I write it? It's just two weeks before Chelsea.' But as soon as I sat down, it came; and Philippe did his usual job of looking at it and playing it immediately and making it sound beautiful.

VS: To excuse you further, weren't you also burdened with conducting that year?

AR: Well, I had to be closely involved in the rehearsals any-way because of the intergenerational chorus – with ages ranging from eight to eighty! I had to be sure that everything was singable. The children were great – they sounded like real children, not choristers. And it was wonderful the way the communities got involved. In fact, in the case of Lichfield, they used the performance to establish a Festival Chorus, some-thing they hadn't had before. But the reason why I did the actual conducting – 'burdened' isn't how I'd put it; it was a pleasure too – was so that the festivals could afford four or five extra musicians for the orchestra. There were money problems that year because of the expense of an orchestra – and although the choruses were amateur, there were quite a lot of choir trainers and accompanists – and of course travel and administration costs. Even with regard to the use of Salisbury Cathedral, we kept wondering: could we manage it or couldn't we? But we had to assume we could; there was no other way to proceed, really.

VS: Since you've touched upon money and festivals, I should say that things for the most part ran smoothly on that front, even if there were some constraints and uncertainties. But the picture would not be complete if I didn't mention one unfortunate exception. The Chelsea Festival wound itself up at the end of year three, and a different organization called the Chelsea Arts Festival took its place. It was only with the greatest of persistence that Philippe received anything at all from them for that fourth year; they still owe him and the pianist more than half their fee. First they claimed that they hadn't received their invoices; then they claimed that they simply didn't have the money. It is painful to see musicians, who aren't rich by any means, being taken advantage of in this way. But, as Philippe says, when he thinks of the project, it is your music rather than this sorry business, isolated as it was, that comes overwhelmingly to mind.

AR: Well, that's one instance, involuntary in this case, of artists having to subsidize their own art. But the project did also benefit from the generosity of a great many people – such as friends of the festivals. And when the three-year guarantee of the funding agencies ran out, it was an anonymous donor who provided the commission fee for the fourth year.

VS: Continuing with the subject of festivals but moving from money matters to logistics, did you find having three performances in different places and on different dates a problem?

AR: In terms of logistics, perhaps – for example, finding dates when all the musicians were available – not just for the concerts, for the rehearsals as well. But in fact it was wonderful to have three performances. It made all the difference to the work. It's true, I could only compose with one venue in mind, and the other two festivals had to find something similar; but that wasn't a serious disadvantage. What was a huge advantage was the chance I got to listen to the music as it was actually being performed and to make changes for the next concert – sometimes just a bit of tweaking, but at other times, as with the violin meditation, a major change. And the performers became more comfortable with the music when they'd played it a couple of times. So by the time the third concert came around, it would still sound fresh, but you could tell they felt at home with it. In a way it's a pity that it's the first performance that gets reviewed! But at least the recording for radio was always done at the third performance, which of course was more polished; and besides, Lichfield Cathedral, particularly the Lady Chapel, has a very good acoustic.

VS: How did your works turn out to be so long – so much longer than the festivals had commissioned?

AR: I got carried away – and they didn't rein me in. Actually, the precedent was set by the first year; once that had turned out all right with the listeners and critics, the festivals weren't too concerned about limiting the length of the works in subsequent years.

VS: Well, why was the first year so long then?

AR: If you'd written me a short libretto, Vikram, twenty minutes' worth, so to speak, that's all I'd have written. But because you weren't given the time to write anything, I had to forage around for something from your work to inspire me. I chose your translations of Du Fu's poems, which turned out to be forty minutes long. So by writing nothing, you doubled the length of my work.

VS: Considering the length of your pieces, there was clearly no room for anything else in the second half of the concerts in which they were played. But what about the rest of the programming – the first half? From our point of view the new piece may have been at the centre of things, but for most of the audience, they were going to a concert which consisted of other things besides.

AR: The programming of a concert is very important – and I admit that in the first year, the first half was a bit ad hoc. *Songs in Time of War* had tenor, violin, guitar and harp – and there wasn't a lot we could choose from with those instruments. We had the Saint-Saëns *Fantaisie* for violin and harp, and Piazzolla's *Café 1930* for violin and guitar. And Mark Padmore sang Vaughan Williams's *Ten Blake Songs* with Gareth Hulse on oboe – though I hadn't used the oboe in my work. At one point, I did think of taking advantage of Gareth by having a few plaintive oboe notes sound offstage at the very end of my piece to represent the ghosts of the dead soldiers in the 'Ballad of the Army Carts'. But in the event, I didn't.

VS: The second year wasn't ad hoc in the least: all Bach and very symmetrical: a motet for double choir – *Singet dem Herrn ein neues Lied*, the Chaconne from the second partita for solo violin, another motet for double choir – *Komm, Jesu, komm*.

AR: I think it was the most successful year as far as programming went. *Shared Ground* and *Ponticelli* were basically inspired by Bach's motets and solo violin music. I really steeped myself in those works that year – I had never written for unaccompanied choir or solo violin before – and I can see a few direct influences here and there. For example, the repeated 'Komm' in *Komm, Jesu, komm* was reflected in my repeated setting of the word 'This' in the last of your poems. And the programme order of the first half established the interlocking of choir and solo violin which we further developed in the *Shared Ground/ Ponticelli* sequence.

VS: The third year, when *The Traveller* was performed, the Britten Sinfonia played Britten's arrangement of the Purcell *Chacony in G*. And Mark Padmore sang Finzi's *Dies Natalis* with them. But the programming that year caused quite a few problems for Philippe, I remember. He had planned a Bach concerto, but because the festivals couldn't afford the expense a harpsichord would entail, that had to be dropped. Also, Richard Hawley at Lichfield, in retrospect quite rightly, though it was quite frustrating at the time, insisted on 'programming that made sense'. Philippe told me that he went back to thinking about solo Bach, then solo Bartók, and finally hit upon Ysaÿe, which was an inspired choice: the second solo violin sonata, with its *Dies Irae* theme in each movement. And that of course made perfect programming sense – *Dies Natalis*, the presence of the *Dies Irae*, and the stages of life and death in *The Traveller*.

AR: Which actually had an effect on my own music in the fourth year, when I incorporated the *Dies Irae* theme in the *Seven Elements Suite* for violin and piano.

VS: Coming to the fourth year then, apart from the *Seven Elements Suite*, you also wrote the *Seven Elements* song-cycle for tenor and piano and *The Hermit on the Ice* for all three. And the all-Schubert first half paralleled this: various songs with some link to each of the seven elements, then the A Major Violin Sonata and finally *The Shepherd on the Rock* in your arrangement for tenor, piano and violin (instead of Schubert's original clarinet).

AR: I learned a lot from doing that arrangement; it's quite a long piece. Getting it into James Gilchrist's range, preventing things from going off the lower range of the violin, and so on – I didn't adapt a lot, but there was a bit of fiddling and fudging, which I hope Schubert wasn't too worried about. The two halves of that programme influenced each other. The very idea for your poem 'The Hermit on the Ice' came from the title of Schubert's piece. And when I was setting the last two lines of your poem – 'The blue earth with its iron core / Spins on through time, spins on through space' – I decided to quote Schubert's lovely floating melody to the words 'und singen . . . und singen' in my violin and piano parts, as I imagined the earth singing Schubert as it spins away into the distance.

VS: We're talking in Salisbury now, in the Old Rectory in Bemerton where, in the early seventeenth century, the poet, musician and priest George Herbert lived and died; and this is where we had many of our earlier discussions about the project, including that crucial one in the red room. And when I've been in India or elsewhere, you've come and stayed here and kept the poetic and musical spirit of Herbert going – and indeed composed quite a lot of these works (as well as others) here. I know that the venue *for* which you compose is very important for your music. But what about the venue *in* which you compose?

AR: It has a huge effect on me. Take the Old Rectory, for example. I love Herbert's poetry. Also, as a teenager, when I had singing lessons, I sang some of Vaughan Williams's settings of Herbert, *Five Mystical Songs*, and I learned quite a lot from that about setting English texts to music. So for me, there was a particular atmosphere to the place where he'd lived. Besides, I loved the peace, the space, the greenery of it. And in practical terms, it was good to be able to spread my keyboard and computer and other equipment around in the red room and work on my music there – and the large table in the kitchen was invaluable when you weren't here and it was uncluttered, especially in the third year when I had all those parts to organize.

But it was in the second year that the sense of place was most critical. The libretto for *Shared Ground* consisted of your poems based on some of Herbert's own poetical forms, and you talk in those poems about your experience of living here. I knew the river that you talked about. I'd been with you when you saw the oak reflected in the flooded glade. It had an enormous effect on my setting of the poems. When you sent them to me from Delhi, I remember I found some of them difficult to set at first – but just being here, I'm sure, got me over some of those difficulties.

VS: Could you give an example or two of these difficulties?

AR: Well, the poem 'And' is so short – it's basically the shortest of the texts. The first time I started looking at the text, I thought, oh, there aren't enough words. I need some more. Then when I looked at it later, what caught my imagination were the words that begin the poem: 'And then I woke.' So what went before? The 'before', of course, was the sleep; the poet was sleeping and dreaming until the word 'And'. And so a lullaby rhythm came to me and a four-note gamelan ostinato. The music to the text itself is shorter than the music of the sleep that precedes it, and then the sleep just creeps back in again at the end of the setting. So I was able in a natural way to make a larger piece out of something quite short. What I used for the wordless sleep bit was the Western tuning equivalent of a Javanese pentatonic mode. Then when he wakes up, and I'm setting the words, I use the star mode. It's quite a sensuous piece.

VS: The star mode? What's the star mode?

AR: Oh, sorry, that's my private way of describing a particular mode I use a lot, which is built up of minor thirds and semitones alternately. I've used it pretty much in every year of 'Confluences'. I first discovered it when I was composing our opera *Arion and the Dolphin*, by piling up alternating fifths and semitones. Then it changed its fortunes and got squished, if you see what I mean.

VS: I think you've lost me, Alec. But to get back to how you disentangle difficulties when composing, I remember you telling me that you had great difficulty working on my poem 'Host', where I talk about the house itself and my sense of Herbert's presence.

AR: Well, I knew the house and its moods, 'Its stones, its trees, its air, / The stream, the small church, the dark rain'. But I just couldn't see, since it was such a personal statement, how I could get a choir to sing it in such a way that it would be intelligible emotionally – or even in terms of projecting the words clearly. Some time later, I happened to go up to London to hear Jeffrey Skidmore and Ex Cathedra (who were going to be our singers that year) perform a piece by Poulenc written around the time Paris was liberated: a most extraordinary work called *Figure Humaine*, set to poems by Paul Éluard. Hearing Poulenc's work inspired me to find a solution to the difficulty of setting your text. I have a solo voice from the choir singing your words as 'the guest', and the choir singing the words of the stones, trees, stream, etc. And the wonderful sonorities of the Poulenc led me to constitute my forces in the same way: to divide the singers into two choirs, each of six voices – soprano, mezzo-soprano, alto, tenor, baritone and bass.

But at the end of my setting, I felt I had left things somewhat up in the air with a single voice; I needed to anchor things, to bring them back to earth – and not just in musical terms. And that's why, immediately afterwards, I had the choir sing Herbert's short poem 'To My Successor', which is inscribed in stone above the porch of the Old Rectory – and which I would never have seen if I hadn't been staying there. I'm glad you let me interpolate it into the text.

VS: Well, it belonged. But I did refuse you permission to use your setting of Herbert's poem 'The Flower' at the very end of the libretto. I didn't want a text by me to close with someone else's words, however much I revered him. What gave you the idea of doing that?

AR: Well, let me go back a bit. You know that that year you gave me the poems for *Shared Ground* very late.

VS: I know. I know. I'm sorry. Muse failure.

AR: Well, I started working on other things. One, of course, was the solo violin pieces for *Ponticelli*. Then Judy* got me involved in the George Herbert hymn-tune project and I decided to set 'The Flower'. That's another thing that wouldn't have happened if I hadn't been here.

   When I'd set it, the tune seemed too good to use only for the hymn, so I adapted it for the second movement of *Ponticelli*. Then, when I had finished both *Ponticelli* and the choral work *Shared Ground* with which it was interlocked, two thoughts struck me. First, it seemed a pity that the violin and the un-accompanied choir were never heard together, and I wondered if I could do something about that. Secondly, the final poem, 'This', is such a bleak poem. And I wanted there to be a sense of hope at the end.

VS: I didn't mind you adding hope, if that was your vision of things, but not with someone else's words!

AR: Yes, I accepted that. So I used the tune of 'The Flower', which I associated with hope, to create an epilogue or coda for

---

* Canon Judy Rees, a friend and neighbour, together with others from the George Herbert in Bemerton Group, encouraged composers to set a number of his poems as hymns, thus adding to the five for which we have well-known and often-sung settings. These nineteen new settings (including 'The Pulley', 'Easter' and 'Christmas') have now been published under the title *Another Music: Through the Year with George Herbert* by the Royal School of Church Music.

violin and choir, but with the choir singing wordlessly. It worked for the audience – and, at the time, for me. But I've been having serious second thoughts about it. I feel it's got to go. Even if the ending is bleak, it's right.

VS: Talking of words, I seem to remember you telling me that you wanted to compose the settings for my words first, and then use those tunes and textures as a source of inspiration for the solo violin pieces of *Ponticelli*. Because I was so late in giving you the words, you had to reverse the order and write the solo violin pieces first. How did that work?

AR: Well, there was a musical logic to what I said, but perhaps I was also just trying to hurry you along. Anyway, I couldn't sit around twiddling my thumbs, so I began work on the *Ponticelli*, the 'little bridges'. I got a lot of inspiration from the five bridges themselves.

VS: I should mention that when you told me about the five bridges in the water-meadow, I was a bit puzzled. I could see what you were referring to as the Arched Bridge and the Flat Bridge – which cross the two branches of the River Nadder – and the Rustic Bridge over the main ditch of the water-meadow – and, at a pinch, the Bridge of Sleepers, which is, well, a sort of half-bridge made of railway sleepers; but your Bridge of Sighs mystified me.

AR [*laughs*]: That was a great discovery. I was walking on the path that goes around the unwooded, open part of the water-meadow. It had just rained, and there was a sort of squelchy area. But I was helped to get across it by what seemed to be a log of wood under part of the path. And when I stepped on it, it made a sort of whooshing, sighing noise. Hence the name. I loved the noise. It only happened after rain. But now, a couple of years later, it doesn't do that any more. And the last time I tried to take that circuit, the swans were nesting there and they hissed me away.

VS: So the Bridge of Sighs has disappeared, perhaps for ever. And all that's left of it is your 'ponticello' of that name.

AR: That's right.

VS: So what did you use for ideas, since you didn't yet have the surrounding poems or their musical settings?

AR: The bridges themselves. For two of them it was the sounds they made – the watery moaning of the Bridge of Sighs, and in the case of the Bridge of Sleepers, the dull plonking noise the individual railway sleepers made when I prodded them with my umbrella – like a giant xylophone. The Rustic Bridge was made of narrow wooden planks, some of which had been replaced with bright new wood. The sequence of old and new wood made an interesting pattern, which I interpreted as musical intervals. The remaining two bridges also provided a visual stimulus in the form of their actual shapes. If you look at my scores you'll see that the opening bars of the music make an image of the Flat Bridge on the page, and the notation of the Arched Bridge music makes an arch shape.

VS: Really, Alec!

AR: Well, you pun quite a lot, so I don't see why I shouldn't – in a musical or a visual sense. Or verbally, for that matter, as with my violinistic title, *Ponticelli*. And, well, Herbert makes lots of puns too – serious puns for the most part – and writes some poems, such as 'Easter-Wings', in unusual shapes. You take your cue for your poem 'Oak' from that. And in fact, in my score of 'Oak', the choir begins by singing wordlessly, and the notation of the music on the page makes an hour-glass shape, mirroring the oak tree and its reflection in the pool below.

VS: Wordplay and shape-play! I'm not sure anyone will take us seriously if they find out how we amuse ourselves.

AR: They can judge the poems and the music on their own merits.

VS: Well, talking of punning, I'm very proud of that particularly puerile pun which came to me out of the blue – and which sums up our collaboration on the project.

AR: 'Seth wrote and Roth set'?

VS: That's the one! But to drift back into seriousness, here's a thought. A writer's book exists once it's written. And it's shared or received when it's read. I don't have to hear or see someone reading it for that to happen. And the process of reading is such a private one. I once came into a room where a friend of mine was reading one of my books, and he clicked his tongue impatiently and shooed me off. But the performance of music is different; it's a public act. And I don't know if a piece of music – or a play for that matter – could be said to be fully realized until it's been performed. I mention this because someone told me many years ago that she'd been at the dress rehearsal of *Arion and the Dolphin*, and she saw you sitting by yourself in tears and asked you if everything was all right. And you'd said, yes, everything was all right; it was just that you'd never really believed that you would hear and see it actually performed, and that that was why you were overcome. I cannot imagine what it must be like to hear your own music for the first time.

AR [*after a pause*]: You know, people assume composers can hear their music in their heads. Well, even if that's true in the abstract, it is the performers who really embody it and bring it to life – in a particular place at a particular time – and let us hear it with our real ears, not those of our minds. It's all the difference in the world. And the audience closes the circle – their attentiveness, their reactions, even the direction of their gaze. When *Songs in Time of War* was performed in Wilton Church, someone said that a veteran from the Second World War had broken down as he listened to 'Moonlit Night'. I was surprised at first, but they told me that he'd said it was exactly as it had been with him, separated as he had been from his wife by the war. To know that your music has moved someone so deeply, what could be a greater reward?

VS: That was the first year of 'Confluences'. I remember there was a long silence before the applause. But more important than the reception and the reviews was the freedom I felt it gave us for the rest of the life of the project. There would be, as you said, no Procrustean constraint on length. A trust had been established – which made everything in the years that followed much easier. Their attitude became, 'Go away and write and compose, we won't bother you.'

AR: Well, the festivals had taken a big risk with us. It was good to feel we hadn't let them down.

Songs in Time of War

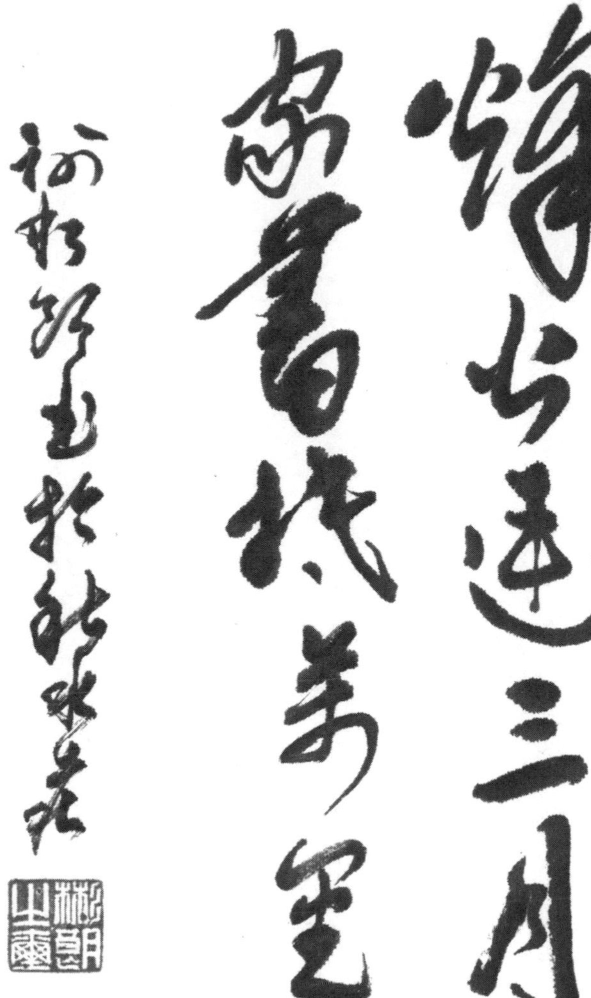
烽火連三月
家書抵萬金

Introduction to

Songs In Time of War

In the first year of the project, by the time we got the go-ahead, I had no time to write anything new, so we decided to make use of something I already had in hand. Alec had earlier set to music some poems on the gardens of Suzhou that I had written while I was a student in China. Now he suggested that he set some translations from the Chinese poet Du Fu that I had done some years later.

I had turned to these poems at a strange time. In my twenties, I had lived in China for two years, studying at Nanjing University, doing research in economics and demography in nearby villages and travelling around the country whenever I got the chance to do so. I grew to love China – in a complex sort of way. In the middle of my time there I hitchhiked home to India via Tibet and wrote an account of this journey, *From Heaven Lake*.

In 1989, the brutal firings on Tiananmen Square took place. For months afterwards I could hardly bear to think of China or Chinese. Then, to my astonishment – for I was in the middle of writing *A Suitable Boy* – I began to translate poems from three of my favourite Chinese poets, Wang Wei, Li Bai and Du Fu.

These three great poets were contemporaries, and lived in the eighth century. Du Fu's poems are, to my mind, the most moving of all. He wrote most of the works presented here during a terrible rebellion in the Tang Dynasty, which caused vast devastation and famine. Du Fu was separated not only from the imperial court, where he was, for a while, an official, but also from his wife and family; he was later to discover that one of his sons had died of starvation.

The Chinese have always turned to their poets for solace in difficult times, so perhaps I should not have been surprised that something drew me back to them in 1989. In 2006, when we were looking for a text, the Iraq conflict was in its third year, and the waste and grief of war gave these poems, more than twelve centuries old, a new charge.

Alec declared my translations singable and arranged them in a different order to create a kind of narrative line, imagining Du Fu alone at night on the boat taking him on his final voyage along the River Yangtze, and reminiscing about family, friends, strangers, country, and the effect on all of them of the civil war. Alec wrote the work for tenor, violin, guitar and harp – to provide what he called an open texture, something less heavy than the piano, the traditional instrument for accompaniment.

We called the work *Songs in Time of War*. Its first performance took place in the beautiful Italianate church at Wilton near Salisbury, close to where Eisenhower, Churchill and others planned their strategy for D-Day during the Second World War.

Songs in Time of War

1. Thoughts while Travelling at Night

Light breeze on the fine grass.
I stand alone at the mast.

Stars lean on the vast wild plain.
Moon bobs in the Great River's spate.

Letters have brought no fame.
Office? Too old to obtain.

Drifting, what am I like?
A gull between earth and sky.

2. Grieving for the Young Prince

From Changan walls white-headed crows took flight
And cawed upon the Western Gate at night –
Then on officials' roofs they pecked and cawed
To warn them to escape the barbarian horde.
The gold whips broke, so hard were they applied.
The exhausted horses galloped till they died.
The court fled, panicked – those they could not find
Of the imperial line were left behind.   ~*

---

* a stanza break at the end of a page is marked by ~
  no stanza break at the end of a page is marked by ⁒

Below his waist, blue coral, glints of jade –
I see a young prince, weeping and afraid
By the cross-roads. Although he won't confess
His name to me he begs in his distress
To be my slave. Thorn scrub he's hidden in
For months has left no untorn shred of skin –
But the imperial nose betrays his birth:
The Dragon's seed is not the seed of earth.

Wolves, jackals roam the city. In the wild
The Dragon and his court remain exiled.
Take care, dear Prince. I daren't speak long with you,
But for your sake will pause a breath or two.

Last night the east wind's blood-stench stained the air
And camels filled the former capital's square.
The Shuofang veterans, bright in their array,
How bold they seemed once, how inane today.
I hear the Son of Heaven has abdicated,
And in the North the Khan, it is related,
And each of his brave warriors slashed his face
– So moved were they by the imperial grace –
And swore to wipe this great dishonour out.
But we must mind our words, with spies about.
Alas, poor Prince, be careful. May the power
Of the Five Tombs protect you hour by hour.

3. *The Visitor*

South and north of my house lies springtime water,
And only flocks of gulls come every day.
The flower path's unswept: no guests. The gate
Is open: you're the first to come this way.
The market's far: my food is nothing special.
The wine, because we're poor, is an old brew –
But if you wish I'll call my ancient neighbour
Across the fence to drink it with us two.

4. *A Fine Lady*

There is a lady, matchless in her beauty.
An empty valley's where she dwells, obscure.
Her family, she says, was once a good one.
She lives with grass and trees now, spent and poor.

When lately there was chaos in the heartlands
And at the rebels' hands her brothers died,
Their high rank failed them, as did her entreaties:
Their flesh and bones remained unsanctified.

The busy world, as fickle as a lamp-flame,
Hates what has had its day or is decayed.
The faithless man to whom she once was married
Keeps a new woman, beautiful as jade.

Those trees whose leaves curl up at night sense evening.
Without its mate a mandarin duck can't sleep.
He only sees the smile of his new woman.
How can he then hear his old woman weep?   ~

Among the mountains, spring-fed streams run clearly.
Leaving the mountains, they are soiled with dross.
Her maid has sold her pearls and is returning.
To mend the thatch they drag the vines across.

Her hands are often full of bitter cypress.
The flowers she picks don't go to grace her hair.
She rests against tall bamboo trees at nightfall.
The weather's cold and her blue sleeves threadbare.

5. Dreaming of Li Bai

The pain of death's farewells grows dim.
The pain of life's farewells stays new.
Since you were exiled to Jiangnan
– Plague land – I've had no news of you.

Proving how much you're in my thoughts,
Old friend, you've come into my dreams.
I thought you still were in the law's
Tight net – but you've grown wings, it seems.

I fear yours is no living soul.
How could it make this distant flight?
You came: the maple woods were green.
You left: the pass was black with night.

The sinking moonlight floods my room.
Still hoping for your face, I stare.
The water's deep, the waves are wide.
Watch out for water-dragons there.

6. Moonlit Night

In Fuzhou, far away, my wife is watching
The moon alone tonight, and my thoughts fill
With sadness for my children, who can't think
Of me here in Changan; they're too young still.
Her cloud-soft hair is moist with fragrant mist.
In the clear light her white arms sense the chill.
When will we feel the moonlight dry our tears,
Leaning together on our window-sill?

7. An Autumn Meditation

I've heard it said Changan is like a chessboard, where
Failure and grief is all these hundred years have brought.
Mansions of princes and high nobles have new lords.
New officers are capped and robed for camp and court.

North on the passes gold drums thunder. To the west
Horses and chariots rush dispatches and reports.
Dragon and fish are still, the autumn river's cold.
My ancient land and times of peace come to my thoughts.

8. The Old Cypress Tree at the Temple of Zhu-ge Liang

Before the temple stands an ancient cypress tree.
Its boughs are bronze, its roots like heavy boulders lie.
Its massive frosty girth of bark is washed by rain.
Its jet-black head rears up a mile to greet the sky.   ~

Princes and ministers have paid their debt to time.
The people love the tree as they did long ago.
The cloud's breath joins it to the long mists of Wu Gorge.
It shares the moon's chill with the high white peaks of snow.

Last year the road wound east, past my old home, near where
Both Zhu-ge Liang and his First Ruler shared one shrine.
There too great cypresses stretched over the ancient plain,
And through wrecked doors I glimpsed dim paintwork and
    design.

But this lone tree, spread wide, root-coiled to earth, has held
Its sky-high place round which fierce blasts of wind are hurled.
Nothing but Providence could keep it here so long.
Its straightness marks the work of what once made the world.

If a great hall collapsed, the oxen sent to drag
Rafters from this vast tree would turn round in dismay.
It needs no craftsman's skills, this wonder of the world.
Even if felled, who could haul such a load away?

Although its bitter heart is marred by swarms of ants,
Among its scented leaves bright phoenixes collect.
Men of high aims, who live obscure, do not despair.
The great are always paid in disuse and neglect.

9. *Spring Scene in Time of War*

The state lies ruined; hills and streams survive.
Spring in the city; grass and leaves now thrive.
Moved by the times the flowers shed their dew.
The birds seem startled; they hate parting too.

The steady beacon fires are three months old.
A word from home is worth a ton of gold.
I scratch my white hair, which has grown so thin
It soon won't let me stick my hatpin in.

10. *To Wei Ba, Who Has Lived Away from the Court*

Like stars that rise when the other has set,
For years we two friends have not met.
How rare it is then that tonight
We once more share the same lamplight.
Our youth has quickly slipped away
And both of us are turning grey.
Old friends have died, and with a start
We hear the sad news, sick at heart.
How could I, twenty years before,
Know that I'd be here at your door?
When last I left, so long ago,
You were unmarried. In a row
Suddenly now your children stand,
Welcome their father's friend, demand
To know his home, his town, his kin –
Till they're chased out to fetch wine in.
Spring chives are cut in the night rain
And steamed rice mixed with yellow grain.
To mark the occasion, we should drink
Ten cups of wine straight off, you think –
But even ten can't make me high,
So moved by your old love am I.
The mountains will divide our lives,
Each to his world, when day arrives.

11. Ballad of the Army Carts

> Carts rattle and squeak,
> Horses snort and neigh –
Bows and arrows at their waists, the conscripts march away.
Fathers, mothers, children, wives run to say goodbye.
The Xianyang Bridge in clouds of dust is hidden from the eye.
They tug at them and stamp their feet, weep, and obstruct
    their way.
> The weeping rises to the sky.
> Along the road a passer-by
> Questions the conscripts. They reply:

They mobilize us constantly. Sent northwards at fifteen
To guard the River, we were forced once more to volunteer,
Though we are forty now, to man the western front this year.
The headman tied our headcloths for us when we first left
    here.
We came back white-haired – to be sent again to the frontier.
Those frontier posts could fill the sea with the blood of those
    who've died,
But still the Martial Emperor's aims remain unsatisfied.
In country after country to the east, Sir, don't you know,
In village after village only thorns and brambles grow.
Even if there's a sturdy wife to wield the plough and hoe,
The borders of the fields have merged, you can't tell east
    from west.
It's worse still for the men from Qin, as fighters they're the
    best –
And so, like chickens or like dogs, they're driven to and fro.

> Though you are kind enough to ask,
> Dare we complain about our task?
> Take, Sir, this winter. In Guanxi

The troops have not yet been set free.
The district officers come to press
The land tax from us nonetheless.
But, Sir, how can we possibly pay?
Having a son's a curse today.
Far better to have daughters, get them married –
A son will lie lost in the grass, unburied.
Why, Sir, on distant Qinghai shore
The bleached ungathered bones lie year on year.
New ghosts complain, and those who died before
Weep in the wet grey sky and haunt the ear.

12. *Thoughts while Travelling at Night*

Light breeze on the fine grass.
I stand alone at the mast.

Stars lean on the vast wild plain.
Moon bobs in the Great River's spate.

Letters have brought no fame.
Office? Too old to obtain.

Drifting, what am I like?
A gull between earth and sky.

Shared Ground

Last night a storm raged round the bare oak tree.
A cold, sharp rain fell; wild in pace
The ice-fed air swirled free.
Now in this place
I see
No trace
Of wind or lee,
No grass, no earth — the space
Is a clear lake, deep as my knee.
I reach its edge and view, far down, my face.

I wade out to the bench, set down my wine,
My bread and cheese, and like some sage
Of old, sit down to dine.
I do not rage
Or pine
At age,
For youth once mine.
This pool, this plate, this page,
This tree whose roots are branch and tine
Holds me in its still hour-glass, its free eye.

Introduction to

Shared Ground

For the second year of the project I moved from China to Europe – from the Tang Dynasty to the Stuarts: to England, to Salisbury, to the very house where the idea for these works had been born, the house where the poet George Herbert had lived and died.

I first came across George Herbert's poetry in *The Albatross Book of Verse*, a popular anthology that had been given to my mother in Darjeeling on her eighteenth birthday; I requisitioned it and took it with me to my boarding school in Dehradun, where I dipped into it from time to time.

When I was seventeen or so, I came to England from India to do my A levels, supposedly in Physics and Mathematics. In the event, I did only one A level: in English. One of our set books was a collection of George Herbert's verse, edited by R. S. Thomas. I still have my copy of that slim volume, published by Faber, and well scored with my earnest and callow notations in red ballpen. I felt a great affinity for Herbert – for his clarity, his depth of feeling, his spiritual struggles (five of his poems are titled 'Affliction'), his delight in the pleasures of nature and music, his wit, his strange juxtapositions, his decorous colloquiality. Though I am neither Christian nor particularly religious, he has remained among my favourite poets.

When, more than three decades later, I heard that his house near Salisbury was on sale, I felt I had to visit it. I had no intention of buying it; I simply wanted to see the place where some of my best-loved poems had been conceived and written. I felt troubled, in fact, that in 1980 the church had sold his Rectory off. If they had to sell something to keep their finances in order, why not sell off a cathedral or two instead of the house of the greatest Anglican poet?

Herbert came from an aristocratic Welsh family; he was Public Orator at Cambridge and had a promising career as a diplomat or courtier ahead of him. Instead, he chose to be a parish priest. The humble parish of Bemerton near Salisbury was offered to him by Charles I 'if it be worth his acceptance'. Herbert found the house in a ramshackle condition, and when, in 1630, he became rector, repaired and expanded it at his own expense. It was to be his only parish; he died of consumption three years later at the age of thirty-nine.

I went down to see the house on an extremely rainy Sunday in June with Philippe and his mother, and immediately fell in love with it. Redone as it was by Herbert himself, it is spacious but not grand – a rectory, not a manor. The garden stretches down to the River Nadder and there is a water-meadow beyond. Though I could not really afford to, I made a bid for it. It struck me that had the house belonged to Donne or Milton or some more overtly forceful personality, I would not have been able to live there. I would either have turned into a ventriloquist's dummy or have ceased to write altogether. But Herbert, for all his depth and richness, is a clear writer and a quiet spirit. He might influence me but would not wish to wrest me from myself.

The Old Rectory faces the very small church of St Andrew's. This is where Herbert preached and from where he tended his small flock of about three hundred souls. One propitious shock I got on that first visit was to see a stained-glass window in the church portraying Herbert holding not a quill or scroll or book – or even, since he was an accomplished musician, a lute or viol – but a violin. In those days, Philippe and I were together, and I took this as a happy sign.

Despite many doubts and difficulties, I did, finally and somehow, manage to buy the house. At first, I used to imagine Herbert writing in his room, looking across towards the church porch – or walking across the fields to Salisbury Cathedral for evensong. After a while, I simply got used to the presence of my tactful host, who never tried to bully me into his philosophy or style. His presence and his poetry were kindly influences. It was not as if, by the nature of his argument, he directly tempered my turmoil; but that through his sense of sympathy and hard-earned stillness he made it more possible to live with it.

Perhaps it was because of this that I was unresistingly drawn into writing a few poems modelled on his verse forms. I was in Delhi at the time I wrote these – I recall street dogs barking late at night – rather than in the green shades of Bemerton: such are the vagaries of inspiration. Though I hope that the mood and spirit of these poems are my own, they are formally based on 'Paradise', 'Easter-Wings', 'Hope', 'Love (III)', 'Virtue' and 'Prayer (I)' – some of the loveliest of Herbert's poems. Since I was inhabiting Herbert's stanzas in both senses of the word, I called my poems *Shared Ground*.

Herbert was a serious poet but fond of wordplay. In 'Paradise', the rhyme-word of the first line in each tercet loses a letter in each succeeding line. In 'Easter-Wings', it appears from recent research (particularly by David West) that the original manuscript lines all ended with the letter E. In 'Prayer (I)', there is no main verb. I have kept to these features. In addition, and I am not quite sure why (except that it seems consonant with Herbert's spirit of simplicity) the poems of *Shared Ground* are all monosyllabic.

The unaccompanied choral settings of the poems alternated

with solo violin movements that Alec collectively called *Ponticelli*. Thus the six pieces of *Shared Ground* were connected by five bridges.

It was the only time in the four years of our collaboration that I did not go to the first performance. I happened to be in Brazil and I decided, instead of returning to England, to go on to Peru. It was not just the attractions of Machu Picchu. These particular and personal poems sung to Alec's music would have overwhelmed me, and the ponticelli played by Philippe, now that we were no longer together, would have brought me to memories and thoughts that would have dyed my mind for days.

Shared Ground

1. Lost

Lost in a world of dust and spray,
We turn, we learn, we twist, we pray
For word or tune or touch or ray:

Some tune of hope, some word of grace,
Some ray of joy to guide our race,
Some touch of love to deuce our ace.

In vain the ace seeks out its twin.
The race is long, too short to win.
The tune is out, the word not in.

Our limbs, our hearts turn all to stone.
Our spring, our step lose aim and tone.
We are no more – and less than one.

There is no soul in which to blend,
No life to leave, no light to lend,
No shape, no chance, no drift, no end.

2. Oak

Last night a storm raged round the bare oak tree.
A cold, sharp rain fell; wild in pace
The ice-fed air swirled free.
Now in this place
I see
No trace
Of wind or lee,
No grass, no earth – the space
Is a clear lake, deep as my knee.
I reach its edge and view, far down, my face.

I wade out to the bench, set down my wine,
My bread and cheese, and like some sage
Of old, sit down to dine.
I do not rage
Or pine
At age,
For youth once mine.
This pool, this plate, this page,
This tree whose roots are branch and tine
Holds me in its still hour-glass, its free cage.

3. And

And then I woke. I tried, once more, to sleep,
But could not coax or keep
The thought of you, your laugh, your hands, your eyes,
Blanked by the sun's calm rise.   ~

The dream was done; your voice was gone; the day
    That rose now, pink and grey,
Was there to work through, till the dark hours came,
    And you, your voice, your name.

4. Host

I heard it was for sale and thought I'd go
    To see the old house where
He lived three years, and died. How could I know
    Its stones, its trees, its air,
The stream, the small church, the dark rain would say:
    'You've come; you've seen; now stay.'

'A guest?' I asked. 'Yes, as you are on earth.'
    'The means?' '. . . will come, don't fear.'
'What of the risk?' 'Our lives are that from birth.'
    'His ghost?' 'His soul is here.'
'He'll change my style.' 'Well, but you could do worse
    Than rent his rooms of verse.'

Joy came, and grief; love came, and loss; three years –
    Tiles down; moles up; drought; flood.
Though far in time and faith, I share his tears,
    His hearth, his ground, his mud;
Yet my host stands just out of mind and sight,
    That I may sit and write.

4a. [Inscription by George Herbert*]

If thou chance for to find
A new house to thy mind
And built without thy cost
Be good to the poor
As God gives thee store
And then my labour's not lost.

* This inscription carved in stone is set into the north wall of the Old Rectory, Bemerton, which was George Herbert's home from 1630 to his death in 1633 and where he wrote much of his poetry.

5. Flash

Bright bird, whose swift blue wings gleam out
As on the stream you dip and rise,
You, as you scan for parr and trout,
       Flash past my eyes.

Bright trout, who glints in fin and scale,
Whose whim is grubs, whose dream is flies,
You, with one whisk of your quick tail,
       Flick past my eyes.

Bright stream, home to bright fish and birds,
A gold glow as the gold sun dies,
You too, too fast for these poor words,
       Flow past my eyes.   ~

But such drab words, ah, sad to say,
When all that's bright has fled and gone,
Praised by dull folk, dressed all in grey,
                    Live on and on.

6. *This*

Hearts-ease, hearts-bane; a balm that chafes one raw;
    The soul in splints; graph with no grid or gauge;
    A fort, a house on stilts, a hut of straw;
A tic, a weal, the flu, the plague, the rage;

Bug swept in through the net; moth with a sting;
    Two planes in fog jammed blind; a mailed kid glove;
    A dance on coals that makes us yelp and sing;
A rook or roc or swan or goose or dove.

A beast of light; a blaze to quench or stoke;
    Bread burst and burnt; sweet wind-fall; storm-cloud-milk;
    Hope raised and razed; skin-ploy; sleep-foil; steel-silk;
Hands held in lieu of breath; our genes' sick joke;
    The sea to drink or sink in; the gods' sty;
    What we must have or die; or have and die.

The Traveller

मैया मैं तो चंद खिलौना लैहौं।
जैसी लोटि धरनि पर मचलौं तेरी गोद न ऐहौं॥
सुरभी को पय पान न करिहौं बेनी सिर न गुहैहौं।
है हैं पूत नंद बाबा को तेरो पूत न कहैहौं॥
आगैं आउ बात पुनि मेरी बलदेवहिं न जनैहौं।
हलि पागमतावति काति लपोमति नई दुलरिया देहौं॥
तेरो तौ मेरो पुनि मैया थोबौं बिमलन जैहौं।
सूरदास है कुटिल नरानी गीत पुमंगल गैहौं॥

Introduction to

The Traveller

The third year, 2008, coincided with the 750th anniversary of the consecration of Salisbury Cathedral; the work we created was to be first performed there. The forces were to be large: a festival chorus of local people (including a separate children's choir), a string orchestra (plus harp and percussion), solo male voice (tenor as usual) and of course solo violin.

I had ranged over China and Europe for the previous two years; the third year brought me home to India. I needed a theme at once grand and intimate – suited to the mood of the cathedral as night fell. Why not all human life?

With this modest thought in mind, I tried to look for a structure for the libretto. I found it finally in the mysterious hymn to creation in the Rig Veda. The hymn has seven verses. Within these seven pillars I nested six arches or zones: the stages of life and death. At Alec's suggestion, I called the piece *The Traveller*, to reflect our earthly journey.

To the four traditional stages of life in the Hindu scheme of things – childhood, youth, adulthood and old age – I added two more: those of the unborn and the dead. I searched for texts in various Indian languages – passages, both sacred and secular, that moved me and that suited these stages.

For example, the first Tamil text from the section on youth comes from an epic poem in which the husband of the heroine Kannagi is wrongly accused of stealing the Queen's ankle bracelet and is put to death. The first part of the extract is from the widowed Kannagi's accusatory lament, and the second from the Queen's premonition of the fall of the kingdom as a result of this injustice. The fury and courage of a young woman confronting the power of the state with the passion and rhetoric of raw grief was what forced this passage upon me. To Kannagi's incantatory speech I added the eerie, almost hallucinatory, vision of the prescient Queen.

I offered a preliminary choice of about twenty such passages to Alec in already existing translations and asked him to tell me which he wanted before I set about retranslating them myself. 'Oh, I want them all,' said Alec.

'But the piece will be an hour long,' I said.

'Well, then, they'll get more than they paid for. But I find all these passages inspiring. I've got to have them.'

So, pondering my tactical unwisdom, I got down to more work than I had bargained for.

The regular Hindi passages presented no serious linguistic problem. Hindi was my first language, and my grandmother insisted that I spoke no other for the first two and a half years of my life. The medieval Hindi of Kabir and the Brajbhasha of Surdas were familiar from literature studies at school as well as from songs. When I began translating the passages from Sanskrit, my long-forgotten schoolboy lessons in that language kicked in. This background helped a little with Pali as well. (There were problems, though, and choices to be made; in Pali, unlike in Sanskrit, the word *deep* is ambiguous, and the Buddha could have been telling his followers either to 'be to yourselves a lamp' or to 'be to yourselves an island'.) I had studied Urdu in order to understand the cultural world of the Muslim characters in *A Suitable Boy*, and had in fact already translated the two Urdu excerpts. When working on the Bengali poem, I was able to draw on the little Bengali that I had gained by osmosis from my mother, who speaks the language fluently. (I regretted, however, that there was no way in English to translate Ramprasad's wonderful pun on 'hope' and 'coming'.) For the texts from Tamil – a Dravidian language with an ancient literary tradition, utterly different from north Indian languages – I was forced to resort to a crib.

Apart from these translations, for each of the six stages of life I wrote a short poem of my own, each with the same number of syllables. The first three have a falling rhythm, and from poem to poem the lines get longer. The last three have a rising rhythm, and from poem to poem the lines get shorter.

My main reward for writing these libretti has always been the music. From the moment in the darkened cathedral that a small bell led into the first verse of the hymn to creation, I was held by the power of it.

> They say love is the reason why
> This soul of ours is bound with bone

could not have been more tenderly set. Nor could Kannagi's demand 'Is there a god?' have resonated with more indignation to the ancient roof and spire.

But the most memorable moment of all was absent; it did not yet exist. It was only created in time for the second performance, and it was wordless: when, towards the end, perhaps at the moment of death, the sound of the violin – 'the traveller', so to speak – wandered above the orchestra, gathering the threads of things that had gone before and weaving them into a meditation of unutterable loveliness, so that I was almost in a trance, only barely conscious that what I was hearing was being produced by human hands, and hands I knew, moving to and fro with one piece of wood against another, causing gentler elements to touch and vibrate and themselves set in motion the invisible, resonant air around.

The Traveller

1.1 Rig Veda 10.129 (Sanskrit, before 1000 BC*)
Creation Hymn Verse 1

There was no being or non-being then,
No world, no sky, no beyond.
What covered it? Where? Who sheltered it?
Was water there, unfathomably deep?

PART I: UNBORN

2. Dhammapada 1.1 (part), 11.146 (Pali, 4th century BC)

The mind precedes all states of being –
They are ruled by the mind,
They are made of the mind.

What is laughter, what is joy
When everything is burning?
Enclosed in darkness
Do you not seek a lamp?

---

* Several of these dates are uncertain.

3. Six Ages: (1) Unborn (Vikram Seth)

Child of son, of daughter,
Tombed and wombed in water,
Flesh to bind and bound me,
Darkness all around me,
Neither seen nor seeing,
Being and not being,
In my world's cessation
Lies my re-creation.

4. Dhammapada 8.100–102 (Pali, 4th century BC)

Better than a thousand meaningless words
Is a single word that brings peace.

Better than a thousand meaningless verses
Is a single verse that brings peace.

And if one should recite a hundred verses,
All filled with meaningless words,
Better is a single word of truth
That brings peace.

Child of son, of daughter . . . &c. [repeat No. 3]

1.2 Rig Veda Creation Hymn Verse 2

There was no death, no immortality,
No sign of night or day.
Windless, that One breathed of its own accord.
Nothing else existed.

PART 2: CHILD

5. Children's Rhyme: Ram Ram Shah (Hindi)

Ram Ram Shah	Ram Ram Shah,
Alu ka rasa	Gravy made from spuds,
Mendaki ki chatni –	Chutney made from female frog –
Aa gaya nasha!	Drink it, and you're drunk!

6. Six Ages: (2) Child (Vikram Seth)

All these colours, named and nameless,
Beings, doings, aimed and aimless,
All these windows, walls and ceilings,
Moon and sun and words and feelings –
All these stars so high above me,
Bright with tears because they love me.

7. Krishna Wants the Moon (Surdas, Brajbhasha, 16th century)

'Mother, give me the moon with which to play
Or I won't come to your lap, but sulk on the ground all day.

I won't drink our cow Surabhi's milk or plait my hair.
I'll just be Papa's boy, and never yours – so there!'

'Listen, son, come closer to me – let's not tell your brother –
I'll get you a nice new bride!' says Krishna's smiling mother.
'Yes, Mother, yes, I swear by you, I'll marry right away.'
The poet adds: 'I'll pose as a guest and sing on that wedding-day.'

Ram Ram Shah . . . &c. [repeat No. 5]

8. The Hope of Hope (Ramprasad, Bengali, 18th century)

To come into this world: a hopeless call,
The hope of hope, that's all.
Like a deluded bee
Trapped on a painted lotus, who cannot struggle free,
So, Mother, am I, and you deluded me.
You called it sugar, while you fed me neem.
My sweet tooth, it would seem,
Has left me with this bitter mouth all day.
Saying to me, 'Let's play,'
Into this world you lured me, and I came.
But Mother, in your game
All happened as you willed
And nothing of my hope has been fulfilled.
Ramprasad says: On the world's scene
What had to be has been.
The evening now has come.
Pick up your child; go home.

All these colours, named and nameless . . . &c. [repeat No. 6]

1.3 Rig Veda Creation Hymn Verse 3

Darkness was covered by darkness in the beginning.
All this was indistinguishable water.
The germ of life, hidden by the void,
That One was brooded into being by heat.

PART 3: YOUTH

9. Dhammapada 18.251 (Pali, 4th century BC)

There is no fire like passion,
No grip like hate,
No snare like delusion,
No river like craving.

10. Shilappadikaram 19.51–59; 20.1–7 (Tamil, 7th century AD)

Are there women here, are there women
Who can bear such injustice to their husbands?
Are there women here? Are there such women?

Are there good men here, are there good men
Who nurture and protect their own children?
Are there good men here? Are there good men?

Is there a god here, is there a god
In this land where the power of the state kills an innocent man?
Is there a god here? Is there a god?   ~

Alas, I saw, I saw in a dream the sceptre and the parasol fall,
The bell by the palace gate toll by itself and resound.

Alas, I saw, I also saw the eight points of the compass waver
And darkness devour the sun.

Alas, I saw, I also saw a rainbow shine by night,
A glowing meteor fall by day. Alas!

11. *Tirukkural 73; 1090; 1201 (Tamil, 4th century AD)*

They say love is the reason why
This soul of ours is bound with bone.

When we drink wine, it gives us joy.
But with love, even the seeing is a joy.

With love, even the memory is sweet,
So love is sweeter than wine.

12. *A couplet (Raheem, Hindi, 17th century)*

Don't break the thread of love, Raheem has said.
What breaks won't join; if joined, it knots the thread.

13. *Six Ages: (3) Youth (Vikram Seth)*

Eyes sealed up with salt and heart charred through with fire,
All my charted days subverted by desire,
Who is this who weeps and who is this who's burning?
Who am I and why – and when am I returning?

1.4 Rig Veda Creation Hymn Verse 4

Desire came then in the beginning,
The first seed of mind.
Poets searching in their heart have found
The bond between being and non-being.

PART 4: ADULT

14. Six Ages: (4) Adult (Vikram Seth)

What can I build or do? What can I shape or form? –
From one and two make four, from cold and cold make warm?
What can I give the world? What can the world give me?
How can I render sight? How can I learn to see?

15. Bhagavad Gita 6.35 (Sanskrit, 2nd century BC to 2nd century AD)

Doubtless, O Arjuna,
The mind is hard to curb and restless;
But by practice and detachment
It can be held still.

What can I build or do? . . . *&c. [repeat No. 14]*

16. Bhagavad Gita 3.8; 18.23 (Sanskrit, 2nd century BC to 2nd century AD)

Perform the right action
For action is better than inaction:
Even the body's journey through life
Could not succeed without action.

The right action, performed without attachment,
Without passion, without hate,
Without desire for its fruits,
That action is called pure.

What can I build or do? . . . *&c. [repeat No. 14]*

*17. Rise Traveller (from the Hymnbook of Gandhi's Ashram,
Hindi, 20th century)*

Rise, traveller, the sky is light.
Why do you sleep? It is not night.
The sleeping lose, and sleep in vain.
The waking rise, and rise to gain.

Open your eyelids, you who nod.
O heedless one, pay heed to God.
Is this your way to show your love?
You sleep below, he wakes above.

Rise, traveller . . . *&c.*   ~

What you have done, that you must bear.
Where is the joy in sin then, where?
When on your head your sins lie deep,
Why do you clutch your head and weep?

Rise, traveller . . . &c.

Tomorrow's task, enact today,
Today's at once; do not delay.
When birds have robbed the standing grain
What use to wring your hands in vain?

Rise, traveller . . . &c.

1.5 Rig Veda Creation Hymn Verse 5

Their cord extended across.
What was above it? What beneath?
There were those with seed, those with powers –
Energy beneath, impulse above.

PART 5: OLD

18. *Dhammapada 18.235 (Pali, 4th century BC)*

You are now like a withered leaf.
The messengers of death are waiting.
You stand at the threshold of departure,
Yet have no provision for the journey.

19. *Six Ages: (5) Old (Vikram Seth)*

My eyes look back at me and say
Where were these wrinkles yesterday?
Where are the friends you used to know?
Where are the oats you used to sow?
Who is this stranger – foolish, wise –
Who stares at you with your own eyes?

20. *Swollen with Pride (Kabir, Hindi, 15th century)*

Swollen, swollen, swollen with pride, you wander.
On your ten months in the womb, why have you ceased to ponder?
Bees store honey, you store gold, but for all you gain here,
Once you're dead, they'll shout, 'Away! Don't let his ghost
   remain here.'
Your wife will follow to the door, your friends to your last station.
Then your soul's alone once more – no friend and no relation.
Burned, your body will turn to ash; buried, you'll lie rotten –
An unbaked water-swollen pot, you'll fall apart, forgotten.
Into the trap the parrot walks, lost in its own confusion.
Into the well of death falls Man, drunk with the world's delusion.

21. *Mahaparinibbana Sutta, from D.xvi.2.25 and 2.26*
(Pali, 5th century BC)

I have now grown old, Ananda, worn out, full of years,
approaching dusk. I am eighty years old. Just as an old cart
is kept going by makeshift repair, so too is it with my body.

Therefore, now, Ananda, be lamps to yourselves. Be a refuge
to yourselves. Seek no other refuge. Take the truth as a lamp.
Take the truth as a refuge. Seek no other refuge.

22. *From a Ghazal (Mir Taqi Mir, Urdu, 18th century)*

All my arrangements were in vain, no drug could cure my malady.
It was an ailment of my heart that made a final end of me.

My term of youth I passed in tears, in age I closed my eyes at last;
That is: I lay awake long nights till dawn and sleep came finally.

1.6 Rig Veda Creation Hymn Verse 6

Who really knows, who can declare
From where this creation came?
The gods themselves came later,
So who can tell from where it rose.

PART 6: DEAD

23. *Six Ages: (6) Dead (Vikram Seth)*

No breath to give or take,
No love to feel or make,
No thought or speech or deed,
No fear, no grief, no need,
No memory, no view,
No four, no three, no two,
No one, no entity
To be or cease to be.

24. Bhagavad Gita 2.11–2.17 (Sanskrit, 2nd century BC to 2nd century AD)

Though you speak words of wisdom,
You grieve for those for whom you should not grieve.
The truly wise grieve neither
For the dead nor for the living.

Never have I not existed,
Nor you, nor these kings,
Nor from this time on
Will we ever not exist.

The embodied self passes through
Childhood, youth, old age;
So does it pass into another body.
This does not perplex the wise.

Cold, heat, joy, sorrow
Come to us through the touch of matter.
What comes and goes is transient.
Arjuna, endure such things.

One whom these do not torment,
Who treats joy and sorrow alike
And is steadfast through all
Is fit for immortality.

What is not does not come to be.
What is does not cease to be.
Those who see the core of things
Know the truth about both these.

That which pervades this universe
Is indestructible.
No one can destroy
What cannot perish.

1.7 Rig Veda Creation Hymn Verse 7

Whence this whole creation has arisen,
Whether it was made or was not made,
He who surveys it from the highest heaven,
Only he knows; or perhaps he does not know.

EPILOGUE

Child of son, of daughter . . . *&c. [repeat No. 3]*

25. *The Meeting Has Dispersed*
(Munshi Amir Ahmad Minai, Urdu, 19th century)

The meeting has dispersed; the moths
    Bid farewell to the candle-light.
Departure's hour is on the sky.
    Only a few stars mark the night.

What has remained will not remain:
    They too will quickly disappear.
This is the world's way, although we,
    Lost to the world, lie sleeping here.

Seven Elements

Introduction to

Seven Elements

For the fourth and final year of the project, we reduced ourselves from the massed forces of the third year to just three performers: violin, tenor and piano. We agreed that there should be a song-cycle for tenor and piano; a suite or sonata for violin and piano; and a concluding piece for all three.

One year had related to China, one to Europe, one to India. But whereas these were zones of culture that I was familiar with, it was not at all clear to me what the theme for the fourth year should be. Various suggestions had been made by various listeners, as we'd hoped: why not try Australia, or Africa, or South America, or the oceans, or even outer space? But nothing seemed to click. I wanted the fourth year to be different somehow – and yet partake of something from the previous years, so that I could have in my text phrases and echoes of what had gone before. Since the first three years had dealt with various geographical spaces, perhaps the fourth could include the aspect of time. Then, I don't know quite how, the idea of the elements struck me, and I began working on a few poems based on these; but very slowly.

Shortly afterwards, I accepted an invitation from a literary festival in Milan: La Milanesiana. Its theme that year happened to be 'The Four Elements'. Alec's deadline was still some months off and I had been dawdling away. But my reading in Milan was due to take place much sooner than that, and this compelled me to write more and to waste my time less. (Not that I think wasting one's time is not a part of writing, but in my case it often seems to be the whole of it.) In due course, my seven poems were ready, all set to be translated into Italian.

But why seven – given only four elements? Well, apart from the four elements in the European tradition – earth, air, fire and water – in India there is a fifth element, a quintessence: space. And the five Classical Chinese elements overlap with these: they are fire, water, earth, metal and wood. By combining the elements of the three culture zones of the previous years, I had the subject for the concluding year. And somehow, through the elements, the oceans and nature and space and time were all included.

The effect of writing these seven poems about the elements was immediate and long-lasting. I began to see the world in sevens. The seven days of the week, the seven notes of the scale, the seven bright stars of the Great Bear, the seven animals that I have recently sculpted in different materials ranging from glass to plaster to wood to stone to steel to bronze to pewter. For some reason, the hotel in which we were housed in Milan had seven square black bottles of shampoo, conditioner, body lotion, hand cream, etc., with the labels Ira, Invidia, Superbia, and so on. This fed into my obsession, and I tried to connect the elements to the deadly sins. Of course, this sort of thing can drive you mad.

All seven poems were first recited in Milan, and published in an Italian newspaper. So, paradoxically, their first ever publication was in the form of a translation. I later showed them to Alec, and he seemed happy with them. He began setting them as his song-cycle. Parallel to these, he began writing his suite for violin and piano in seven movements, influenced both by the themes of the songs and by the music of the previous years.

The programming for the first half of the concert was planned to include seven Schubert songs loosely relating to the seven elements, followed by his entrancing 'The Shepherd on the Rock' in a transcription by Alec for tenor, piano and violin (in lieu of clarinet). So, by way of a parallel coda, I wrote an eighth poem which included all the seven elements and called it 'The Hermit on the Ice', to be set for the same performers.

Things seemed to be going along swimmingly and I was congratulating myself on having finished my work on the entire project when I got a plaintive email from Alec.

One of the poems that had so pleased the Milanese audience did not please him at all. He liked the other six poems. But he couldn't do anything with 'Fire'.

'What's the matter with it?' I asked.

'Well, nothing really . . . I mean, everything.'

'So you don't like it?'

'Oh, I like it a lot . . .'

'Alec, you're talking in riddles.'

'It's just that it's a bit literary and, you know, indirect. The other poems I can work with.'

'And this one?'

'Fine as a poem, useless as a text.'

After a while he added, 'Couldn't you just go back and write something else?'

No, I said, I couldn't. This was the fruit of my inspiration. I couldn't go back to the muse and say, sorry, you've done your best and I've done my best, but my composer (who actually likes the poem) has nevertheless rejected our work. I was, in fact, quite annoyed. By now I had moved on and was working on other things. I couldn't revert to the elements just to appease a fussy composer.

But upon looking at the poems, I began to think that maybe Alec had a point. The other six poems – 'Earth', 'Air', 'Wood', 'Metal', 'Water' and 'Space' – related to their elements directly. In the case of 'Fire', however, I had worked much more metaphorically. I had used the sun and the moon as symbols of fire – and then used two characters to refer to these: one from Indian religious poetry, the infant Krishna; and the other from European drama, Oswald in Ibsen's *Ghosts*. This made things difficult for the audience – especially since everything was being sung. When reading a poem, you can slow down or even go back if you don't understand a reference, but you can't do the same when you're listening to a song. Alec was right; the poem wouldn't work.

But what could I do? Time was short, and I couldn't see how the same poet, within a couple of months, could write two completely different poems on the same subject and with the same title.

Eventually, as the deadline approached, Alec told me that the paradox was easily soluble. He suggested I go home and get drunk. This irresponsible advice worked. The muse – or maybe a different muse – re-emerged, not unwillingly, from the fumes of the wine, and the second poem, also called 'Fire', was born. I still don't know what to think of this particular poem, which is different from anything I have ever written. It sits in the middle of the libretto, and Alec has set it to some of his craziest music. But here is the rejected poem, which, though deprived of music, should not, I feel, be thereby deprived of existence.

Fire (1)

Mother, give me the moon.
I want it as my toy.
Mother, I want it soon
Or I'll be Papa's boy.

No, I won't plait my hair.
I won't go out to play.
I'll sulk on the ground all day.
I won't come to your lap – so there!
Nor will I drink this milk from Surabhi, our cow.
Mother, I want the moon – and I want it now.
Here in this bucket filled with water it scatters.
But that one there never shatters,
Cold in its silver fire,
Climbing higher and higher.
I now know, Mother,
You only love Balram, my brother,
Who loves to drive me wild.
He says you bought me, that I'm not your child.
No, don't sing me a tune.
Mother, give me the moon.
The moon, the moon.

Mother, give me the sun.
The horror, the horror has begun.
For ten years now my father has been dead.
This is his heritage, here in my sick head.
Who will rid me of my fear?
Regina would, her health and strength and cheer –
But she has gone and never will return.
Now everything will burn.
The orphanage has been consumed by fire.
My body is the wreckage of desire.
I burn, I burn away.
I'll lie like this for years, helpless and old and grey.
I didn't ask for life. I never sleep.
No, Mother, do not weep.

Help me to end my endless night.
The sunlight on the ice, this morning light.
I am cold. It is done.
Mother, give me the sun.
The sun, the sun.

Seven Elements

1. Earth

Here in this pot lies soil,
In which all things take birth.
The blind roots curve and coil
White in the sunless earth.
The soil slips over fire.
The great lands crack apart
And lava, pulsing higher,
Springs from earth's molten heart.

Here in this jar lies clay,
Dried clay, a whitened dust.
The moistened fingers play
To make it what they must.
The earth begins to reel,
Round, round, and near and far,
And on the potter's wheel
Is born another jar.

Here in this urn lies ash,
Dust uninfused with breath:
Burnt wood, burnt bone, burnt flesh,
The powdered clay of death.
The embers from the pyre
Sink on the rivered earth
And moistened into mire
Wait for a further birth.

2. Air

Air from your lips makes me vibrate,
Who am a tube of air,
And I make ripples where
Singing, singing,
I speak of joy and soothe the erratic pulse of hate.

Air from the sky slips past my arms
And buoys my tube of air
And thrusts me forward where
Winging, winging,
I soar above all earthly frenzies and alarms.

I am the stuff of death and birth,
Of wreck and of repair,
The unseen skin of air –
Clinging, clinging
To wrap and save for life the injured crust of earth.

3. Wood

A wooden bench. A wooden cuckoo-clock.
A pencil marks the surface of a pad.
Outside, a woodpecker goes pok-pok-pok.

A girl plays with a carved owl on a swing.
A log-pile lies beside a wooden bridge.
Listen: a bamboo flute begins to sing.

Some find the song too sad or too oblique.
I hear a wooden drumbeat sound from far.
The oak stirs in the wind; its branches creak.

~

The rains will come. The swing will rot and fray.
The logs will burn. The bench will crack and split.
The owl will break. The girl will move away.

The oak will die. The bridge will fall apart.
The cuckoo-clock and flute and drum will fade
But pok-pok-pok will echo in her heart.

As for myself, the nest is in my head.
The eggs are laid. The hatchlings will emerge
And pok-pok-pok will echo when I'm dead.

4. *Fire*

Fa-yaah
O fayah – fayah – fayaaah
Dizayaah
Hot hot hot
I'm burning a lot with dizayaah
O fayah fayah fayah
Hot as a filament wa-yah
Hot as prawn jamba-la-yah
I'm burning so hot
I'm baking a pot –
O hot hot hot as dizayaah
Fa-yaah! Fa-yaah!

All was born from me –
All your eyes can see.
Who gave life and birth
To sun and star and earth?

Who gave pulse and germ
To man and beast and worm?
Who is hot hot hot
When black space is not?
Who is bright bright bright
In this endless night?
Fa-yaah! Fa-yaah! Fa-yaah!

Fa-yaah
O fayah – fayah – fayaaah
Dizayaah
Hot hot hot
I'm burning a lot with dizayaah
O fayah fayah fayah
Hot as a funeral pa-yaah
Leaping up ha-yaah and ha-yaah –
I sizzle, I daze,
I fizzle, I blaze,
I scorch, I toast,
I smoulder, I roast,
I flare, I excite,
I flash, I ignite,
I rage, I lust,
I blaze, I combust,
Red, yellow, white,
I light up the night,
This endless night, with dizayaah,
O fa-yaah! Fa-yaah! Fa-yaah!

5. Metal

A steel tube on steel wheels upon steel rails.
A steel nib moves black fluid on the page.
Across from me sits a woman sadly looking
At the gold ring on her finger.
Around her neck is a gold chain with a cross.
She takes her mobile phone out of her bag
And taps its shining keys.

An aluminium tube thrust through the air.
Clunk goes my safety belt as I unclip it.
Near me tapping titanium keys
Sits a man in thought. From time to time he grips
The can of beer perched at the edge of his table.
He ignores the time on his screen and looks
At the platinum watch on his wrist, then out at the broad wings
That slice the sunset in two –

Cadmium red and orange, cadmium yellow and lemon.
Look, look, their tears fall down like mercury.
Trapped in their public and metallic zones,
On wheels, on wings, how can they shield their hearts
From the compulsive radium of love –
Or is it tarnished silver?

6. Water

The moon bobs in the river's spate.
The water's deep, the waves are wide.
Around my house lie springtime floods.
My friend and I drink tea inside.

Du Fu is singing at the mast.
Li Bai lies in his watery grave.
Far far away, on alien shores
The lashing breakers mourn and rave.

The hermit sits upon the ice.
The ice-bear moves from floe to floe
And from the hot spring newly bathed
Snow monkeys roll upon the snow.

The clouds disperse, the ropes thaw out.
Ice tinkles down from frozen sails.
The ocean churns and treasures rise:
Ambrosia and minke whales.

Slivers of ice brush past my face
As I swim in the icy bay.
A rumbling glacier calves a berg.
The watery sun shoots forth a ray.

The turbined vessel steams and steers
But cannot veer around the ice.
The beavers build but cannot dam
The stream that flows through Paradise.

Water destroys the unbaked pot.
Water is magicked into wine.

Water dissolves the fabled salt
And sinks the lover in the Rhine.

If only I were wine instead
Of water and my breath a cloud,
Of man's last disobedience and
This brittle world I'd sing aloud.

O water-being, drunk with gain,
Mere water are your brains and blood
And water are your flesh and tears
And water is the coming flood.

The ice-caps melt, the ports are drowned.
The current from the gulf is still.
The darkening planet drinks the sun
And cyclones swirl and whirl and kill.

Where are the islands of delight?
Where are the fields that now are dust?
Where is the crop of measured years?
I weep, I weep because I must.

The moon bobs in the river's spate.
The water's deep, the waves are wide.
Around my house lie springtime floods.
My friend and I drink tea inside.

My friend and I drink tea and wine.
Upon the pane our breath is steam.
Our tears flow down from grief and joy.
We dream and drink, we drink to dream.

7. *Space*

Space springs the stars apart.
Space fills the neutron's heart.
Air, water, earth, no less,
Are thin with emptiness.
We are such space-filled stuff,
How could we be enough
To be or touch or do,
To track black holes or view
Bright galaxies or trace
Dark matter spun through space?

To sense it, must we first
Return to space, dispersed? –
No soul in which to blend,
No life, no light to lend,
No breath to give or take,
No love to feel or make,
Stirless in zero space,
No entity, no place,
Ordained to retrogress
To shreds of nothingness.

THE HERMIT ON THE ICE

The hermit sits upon the ice.
The bluish light burns all around,
Immune to flame and sacrifice,
To breath and death and scent and sound.

The scent of pine, the river's roar
Are muted in his breath and pace.
The blue earth with its iron core
Spins on through time, spins on through space.

Note on Calligraphy by the Author

Songs in Time of War

The larger Chinese characters, to be read in vertical columns from right to left, are taken from Du Fu's poem 'Spring Scene in Time of War':

> The steady beacon fires are three months old.
> A word from home is worth a ton of gold.

Literally:

> beacon fire connect three month
> home letter worth 10,000 gold

The smaller characters – or colophon – without which the work would not be complete, state: 'Written by Xie Binlang at Autumn Waters Manor.'

Xie Binlang is my Chinese name, an emulation of Vikram Seth, with the surname first; Autumn Waters Manor is the name that was humorously given to the Old Rectory by my calligraphy teacher of many years, Zhao Yizhou, on his first visit there. It's a pun: the title of my favourite (and the most whimsical) chapter in Zhuangzi's philosophy is 'Autumn Waters'; and 'manor' has the same Chinese character as 'Zhuang'.

The style of the calligraphy is xing-cao or 'running cursive'.

The impression of the seal is red in the original work. The seal itself was carved by the late Zha Zhonglin.

Shared Ground

This is the handwritten poem 'Oak', which emulates the printed form of George Herbert's poem 'Easter-Wings'.

(In the first edition of 1633, and each subsequent edition, the poem has the shape of two hour-glasses. In the manuscript in the Dr Williams's Library in London, it has, far more aptly, given the words of the poem, the shape of two larks.)

The Traveller

These eight lines handwritten in Brajbhasha, a variant of Hindi, are the poem by Surdas, 'Krishna Wants the Moon'.

Seven Elements

This roundel is written in Arabic – which, like Chinese, represents one of the world's great calligraphic traditions. I studied Arabic calligraphy in the thuluth script for a few months with my teacher Nassar Mansour.

The numerals at the foot of the roundel indicate the year 1432, which in the Islamic calendar corresponds to 2011. In the image I have combined the words for the seven elements with seven bright stars in the night sky.

VS

Arched Bridge